COUNTRIES IN OUR WORLD

IRAQ

Susan Crean

W
FRANKLIN WATTS
LONDON•SYDNEY

First published in 2009 by
Franklin Watts
338 Euston Road
London NW1 3BH

Franklin Watts Australia
Level 17/207 Kent Street
Sydney NSW 2000

Produced for Franklin Watts by
White-Thomson Publishing Ltd
+44 (0) 845 362 8240
www.wtpub.co.uk

Series consultant: Rob Bowden
Editor: Sonya Newland
Designer: Alix Wood
Picture researcher: Amy Sparks

A CIP catalogue record for this book is available
from the British Library.

Dewey Classification: 915.67

ISBN 978 0 7496 8848 6

Printed in Malaysia

Franklin Watts is a division of Hachette
Children's Books, an Hachette UK company

www.hachette.co.uk

Picture Credits
Corbis: Cover (Hassan Ali/epa), 4 (Nico Tondini/
Robert Harding World Imagery), 6 (Nico Tondini/
Robert Harding World Imagery), 8 (Reuters), 9
(Ed Kashi), 11 (Nik Wheeler), 12 (ATEF HASSAN/
Reuters), 13 (Reuters), 14 (Jerome Sessini), 17
(Alaa Al-Shemaree/epa), 19 (Ahmad Yusni/epa),
20 (David Butow), 23 (Faleh Keiber/epa), 24 (Thaier
Al-Sudani/Reuters), 25 (Peter Andrews/ Reuters).
Fotolia: 1 (Morane), 16 (Morane). **Photoshot:** 7,
10 (World Pictures). **US Army:** 18 (Capt. Robin
Worch). **US Department of Defense:** 15 (LCPA Joel A.
Chaverri), 21 (Petty Officer James Wagner), 22 (Staff
Sgt JoAnn S. Makinano), 26 (Sgt. Gustavo Olgiati),
27 (Sergeant Michael Kropiewnicki), 28 (Master Sgt.
Mike Buytas), 29 (Mass Communication Specialist 2nd
Class James Wagner)

Contents

Iraq has a long and rich history. People have lived there for thousands of years, and organized communities have existed there since about 3000 BCE. These are some of the oldest human settlements that we know of, so Iraq is often called the 'cradle of ancient civilization'.

Where in the world?

Located in the Middle East, Iraq is mostly landlocked, but a 58-km (35-mile) stretch borders the Persian Gulf in the south-east. Iraq is slightly smaller than Sweden and is about the same size as the US state of California. It is bordered by six countries: Iran, Jordan, Kuwait, Saudi Arabia, Syria and Turkey.

The Islamic Empire

The early history of Iraq is closely related to that of its neighbours. These countries formed part of the Islamic Empire, which was established in the area around CE 632 and existed until the end of World War I in 1918. The people of the Islamic Empire followed the teachings of the Islamic (Muslim) prophet Muhammad.

▼ *Iraq has only one sea border – a small stretch of coast on the Persian Gulf.*

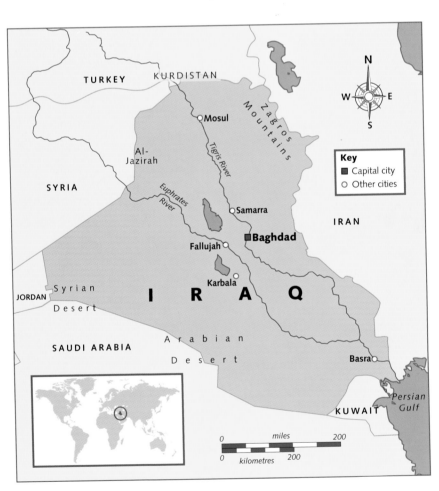

◀ The Malwiya Tower in Samarra, Iraq, was built in the ninth century. It is part of a mosque that was once the largest in the world.

IT STARTED HERE

Language

The Sumerians are the first known civilization to have existed in Iraq. They developed one of the earliest systems of writing and spoke the oldest known language. The Sumerians used this language until 2000 BCE, when a group called the Akkadians invaded and replaced the Sumerian language with their own.

British influence

The region that is now Iraq was important to Britain because it lay along a key route to India, which was a British colony. The discovery of oil in the area in 1908 made it even more significant. When World War I broke out in 1914, the British went to Basra, a province in Iraq, and seized the area from its rulers. At the end of the war, Britain remained in Iraq to help it create its own government. Three regions – Mosul, Baghdad and Basra – were merged into one country.

Modern Iraq

In 1921, a monarchy was established to rule over Iraq, but it did not become a fully independent country until 1932. It was ruled by kings until 1958, when the army overthrew the monarchy and declared Iraq to be a republic – a type of government in which the leaders are chosen by the people. Before long, however, it became clear that the Iraqi army was the real leader, and a series of army generals ruled the country rather than allowing people to elect its leaders.

▲ *Iraq's capital city, Baghdad, on the banks of the River Tigris, blends the old with the new.*

The Iran-Iraq War

In 1979, Saddam Hussein became president of the Republic of Iraq. He destroyed Iraq's relationships with many countries – for example, in 1980 Saddam ordered the invasion of Iran, Iraq's neighbour to the east. For eight years the two countries fought a brutal war, during which other Arab countries and the USA supported Iraq. The war ended in 1988 when both sides agreed to stop fighting. Iraq suffered greatly during the war, and at the end it owed a lot of money to the countries that had supported it. This meant there was little money to help rebuild the country.

The First Gulf War

Saddam Hussein blamed Kuwait, to the south-east of Iraq, for his country's problems, claiming that it had taken oil from Iraq. In 1990, Saddam ordered Iraqi forces to attack Kuwait. The rest of the world warned Iraq to leave Kuwait or face war, but Saddam ignored them. Arab countries such as Syria, Saudi Arabia and Egypt worked with the USA and the UK to try to force Iraq from Kuwait. In 1991, international troops attacked Iraq and freed Kuwait, but Saddam Hussein remained in power. He continued to ignore international laws.

BASIC DATA

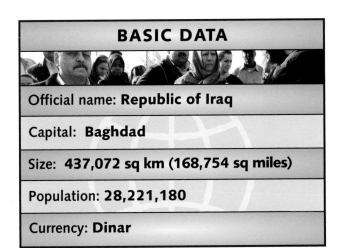

Official name: **Republic of Iraq**

Capital: **Baghdad**

Size: **437,072 sq km (168,754 sq miles)**

Population: **28,221,180**

Currency: **Dinar**

The invasion of Iraq

Saddam's policies resulted in a US-led invasion in March 2003, and he was removed as leader. On 28 June 2004, Iraq again became an independent country. Since then, the USA and other countries have kept many troops in Iraq. Some are still fighting as part of the war effort, and others are there to help keep Iraqis safe from the violence that still occurs between different groups.

▼ *American tanks roll through a deserted street in Iraq during the invasion of 2003. Troops from the USA and the United Nations are still present in the country.*

Landscapes and environment

In the centre and south-eastern parts of Iraq are wide plains with many lakes. Between the two main rivers north of here is a plateau called Al-Jazirah. In the west is a vast desert area and in the north-east are highlands and mountains.

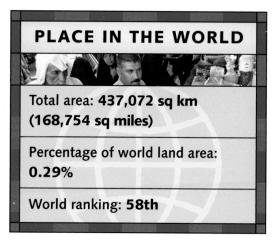

PLACE IN THE WORLD

Total area: **437,072 sq km (168,754 sq miles)**

Percentage of world land area: **0.29%**

World ranking: **58th**

Land of two rivers

Iraq's two main rivers, the Tigris and the Euphrates, are among its most important features. Both rivers start north of Iraq, in Turkey, and the Euphrates also flows through part of Syria. The entire area is known as Mesopotamia, which means 'between the rivers' in Greek. Along the valleys of these rivers is a rich, flat, central plain. This region is called the Fertile Crescent.

Fresh water in Iraq

People in Iraq try to control how much water is available by building dams and reservoirs. Because the Tigris and Euphrates flow through Turkey and Syria before they reach Iraq, Iraq's water supply depends on what happens in these countries. Both Syria and Turkey have built their own dams along the two rivers, and as more dams are built upriver, Iraq's water sources shrink.

▼ *An Iraqi fisherman casts a net into the 2,700-km (1,700-mile) Euphrates River.*

▲ *In the north-east, Iraq shares the Zagros mountain range with its neighbour Iran.*

Weather

Much of Iraq has a climate similar to that of the US state of Texas. Winters are mild, while summers are dry, hot and cloudless. Iraq gets some of the hottest temperatures in the world. In the summer, temperatures are often over 38°C (100°F). In the northern mountainous regions winters are cold with occasional snowfall, and summers are cool. When the snow melts in the spring, it can lead to flooding in central and southern Iraq. The Syrian Desert gets almost no rainfall and most of Iraq has less than 25 cm (10 in) of rain each year.

IT'S A FACT!

The Iraqi capital, Baghdad, has an average of 154.8 mm (6.1 in) of rain each year – much less than the world average of 857 mm (33.7 in). Australia has the least rainfall of all the continents except Antarctica, but even Australia's driest city, Adelaide, has more than three times as much rainfall as Baghdad!

Iraq's marshlands

A low-lying area that was once marshland borders the Persian Gulf in Iraq. For more than 5,000 years the Marsh Arab people lived in this region, and it was known as a key stop for hundreds of species of migrating birds. In the 1990s, the Iraqi government ordered the marsh to be drained as a punishment to the half-million Marsh Arab people who opposed Saddam Hussein's rule. The government built dams and drained the land of its water. This destroyed the ecosystem, and the marshlands became mostly desert. Today, Iraqis are slowly restoring the marshlands, and in 2003 a group broke down dams that had been built to stop water from flowing there. About 20 per cent of the original marsh was re-flooded. Thousands of birds have returned to the region, as have thousands of Marsh Arab people.

THE HOME OF...

Oil

Iraq's oil supplies are the third largest in the world, after Iran and Saudi Arabia. Iraq has a supply of 115 billion barrels of oil, but oil production has slowed because of war. Iraq produces an average of two million barrels per day. This is less than that produced by countries such as Russia, the USA and Mexico.

Wildlife in Iraq

Animals found in Iraq include the cheetah, gazelle, antelope and hyena. War has harmed Iraq's animals as well as its people, and the country has lost much of its wildlife as a result. For example, thousands of seabirds died due to damaged oil wells during the Gulf War.

◀ Some historians believe the area of Iraq where the Marsh Arabs live was the site of the so-called 'Garden of Eden' mentioned in the Bible.

▲ *Most of Iraq is desert, but plants such as palm trees grow along the banks of the Euphrates (above) and Tigris rivers.*

Desert regions

Despite its fertile central plain, much of Iraq is desert. West of the Euphrates lies the harsh environment of the Syrian Desert, and to the south-west is the Arabian Desert. Because it is mostly desert, there is little vegetation in Iraq, and only about 13 per cent of the land can be used for agriculture. Roughly 10 per cent of the land is used for grazing.

IT'S A FACT!

The Syrian Desert covers about 260,000 sq km (100,000 sq miles) of Iraq, Syria, Jordan and Saudi Arabia. It is four times the size of the Mojave Desert in the south-western USA. The Sahara Desert in Africa – the world's biggest – is 35 times larger than the Syrian Desert.

Population and migration

Around 75 to 80 per cent of Iraq's population is Arab and 15 to 20 per cent is Kurdish. The Kurds are an ethnic population of what were once nomadic people. The ethnicity of Arabs is based on language – simply put, an Arab is any person who speaks Arabic.

PLACE IN THE WORLD

Population: **28,221,180**

Percentage of world total: **0.42%**

World ranking: **42nd**

Settlement

Iraq's geography has largely influenced where Iraqis live. For example, people do not live in Iraq's deserts, which are uninhabitable. Instead, they live in the country's central, fertile valley. Many Arabs in Iraq are the descendants of peoples who have lived in this region for centuries. Today they mainly live in cities, such as Baghdad (5.1 million), Mosul (1.3 million) and Basra (0.9 million). These are the capital cities of the provinces of the same name. There are around 20 cities with more than 100,000 inhabitants each, situated along Iraq's Tigris and Euphrates rivers.

◀ *Iraqi men and women shop for food at a market in Basra, the third most populated city in Iraq.*

The Kurds

Most of Iraq's Kurdish population live in the north of the country, in the mountainous area that borders Turkey, Iran and Syria. A total Kurdish population of 25 million spills into all these countries. The area where Kurdish people live is called Kurdistan, but although it has its own name, it is not a country in its own right. The Kurdish part of Iraq is an autonomous region, which means it has a degree of self-rule, but the parts in Iran and Syria are not recognized internationally in this way. The Kurdish people are the largest ethnic group in the world without their own country.

▼ *A Kurdish family sits on a hilltop near their village of Rahima Quta in northern Iraq. The Kurds have been fighting for their own country for many years.*

A hard life

The Iraqi people have faced many hardships, partly due to the rule of Saddam Hussein and partly because of the long years of war. As a result, the population has changed. More than five million Iraqis – one in five of the total population – are refugees or displaced persons. They have been forced from their homes due to the violence in their country. More than 80 per cent of refugees are women and children.

Iraqi refugees

Around two million people have left Iraq for other countries, mostly in the Middle East. Many others remain in Iraq but have had to flee their homes, jobs and friends in fear of their lives. Sixty per cent of refugees hope to return to their homes one day. At the same time, some Iraqis who had left before the US invasion returned to Iraq after Saddam Hussein was removed from power. Refugees often live a hard life: they have no permanent home and they are not allowed to work in most host countries in which they settle. They have difficulties finding shelter and food, as well as in gaining access to healthcare and education.

GOING GLOBAL

Many Iraqis are refugees who have fled violence in their homeland. These include 500,000 in Syria, 450,000 in Jordan, 300,000 in the USA, 250,000 in the UK and 135,000 in Iran. About half of the refugees have gone to neighbouring countries – mainly Syria and Jordan. It is difficult for these countries to support the Iraqis, though, and they do not encourage new refugees.

▼ *These Iraqi refugees are waiting to be registered in Syria, where they have fled from the war.*

The impact of war

No one knows for sure how many Iraqis have been killed as a result of internal conflicts and the war. Some groups estimate that the death toll between March 2003 and August 2007 was more than one million Iraqis. Every family in Iraq has been affected by the war: one in four Iraqis has had a family member killed and one in three has had family members leave the country. Today there is almost no immigration into Iraq, and the population growth of Iraq is helped almost solely by new births. An average Iraqi family has four children.

 War has disrupted the lives and neighbourhoods of most Iraqis. This picture shows a rocket attack on a neighbourhood in Fallujah.

IT'S A FACT!

The average lifetime of a person living in Iraq is 69.62 years. By comparison, the average lifetime of a person in France is more than 80 years. The war has caused a public-health crisis in Iraq, and as a result, life expectancy is lower than it was 20 years ago.

Before 1991, the Iraqi people had one of the highest standards of living in the Middle East. War has reduced this, but other countries are trying to help rebuild Iraq. Between 2004 and 2007, £17 billion was promised by other countries. International aid agencies are working to help the Iraqi people overcome some of the difficulties they face.

Religion

Most Iraqis are Muslim. In the Islamic religion as a whole, the largest group are the Sunni Muslims, but in Iraq only about 35 per cent of the population is Sunni. The other key group is Shia Muslims, and about 65 per cent of Iraqis belong to this group. Although Sunni Muslims and Shia Muslims have similar beliefs, they have different political ideas about how a Muslim community should be led. Even so, Shia and Sunni groups have lived side by side in Iraq for centuries, and it is common for Sunni and Shia Muslims to marry each other or to be friends. Today in Iraq, however, some Shia and Sunni Muslim groups are in conflict.

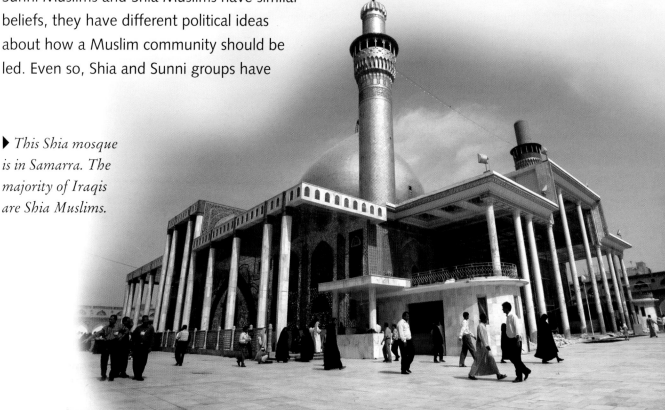

▶ *This Shia mosque is in Samarra. The majority of Iraqis are Shia Muslims.*

GOING GLOBAL

Karbala, in southern Iraq, is one of the holiest cities for Shia Muslims. In 2008, nine million Shia pilgrims travelled to Karbala to visit an important religious site. As many as 80,000 of the pilgrims were non-Iraqis. This was one of the largest pilgrimages in the world.

Festivals

Festivals in Iraq are usually religious. They are the same festivals celebrated by Muslims all over the world. The Arabic word *Eid* means 'festival'. Eid ul-Fitr is the Festival of the Fast Breaking, which marks the end of Ramadan, a month of fasting. During Ramadan, Muslims do not eat or drink anything during the day. They pray and read the Koran. Food and family are important to many religious festivals in Iraq. During Eid al-Adha, the Festival of Sacrifice, people visit relatives – starting with their parents, then the rest of their extended family and friends. Giving meat to people is an important part of this festival.

▲ *Karbala is an important religious site for Shia Muslims. These worshippers pray near the tomb of Imam Hussein, an important figure to Shia Muslims.*

Pilgrimages

Some festivals include a pilgrimage, where people travel to a special place. During Eid al-Adha, Muslims travel to Mecca, in Saudi Arabia, which is Islam's holiest city. Many travel from Iraq, but they come from all over the world. Some airlines even have special rates for Muslims going to Mecca. The pilgrimage attracts millions of Muslims each year.

Life today

Family life for most ordinary Iraqis has been severely disrupted, first by war and now by violence between different local groups. In places that are the most dangerous, including Baghdad, people often stay at home or do not venture far from it. Power cuts are common. Clean drinking water is not always available, and people regularly suffer from food shortages. Parents think about how to feed their family and stay safe. Many men have died in the years of violence and life is even more difficult for their widows, who have to take care of children on their own.

▼ *Education is important to Iraqis. Some parents kept their children home from school when the violence was at its worst, but many children are now returning.*

At the table

The Iraqi diet draws from the rich 'Garden of Eden' foods – so-called because Iraq is thought to be the location of the Garden of Eden described in the Bible. These foods include dates, figs, aubergines, vine leaves and lemons. Rice and grains are also an important part of the Iraqi diet. Iraqis like to flavour foods with herbs such as mint, thyme and dill, and spices such as coriander, cumin, cloves and cinnamon.

IT'S A FACT!

In most European countries and the USA, almost 100 per cent of adults can read. In Iraq, just under 75 per cent of adults can read. Only about 65 per cent of Iraqi women can read, because girls in Iraq often do not receive the same level of education as boys.

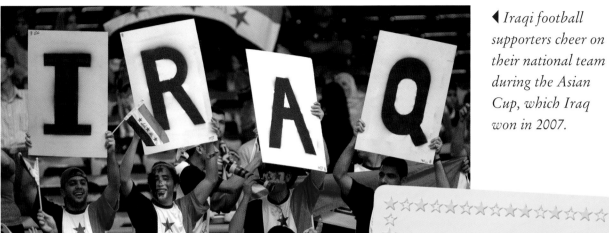

◀ Iraqi football supporters cheer on their national team during the Asian Cup, which Iraq won in 2007.

Modern media

Despite the fact that many Iraqis are confined to their homes, they still have access to dozens of television and radio stations. Al Jazeera is the best-known news channel in the Arab world. Western news is also available in Iraq, such as the BBC. In addition, the USA has backed a television station called Al-Hurra TV and two radio stations. There are about 54,000 Internet connections in Iraq. Many of them are used by officials, but others who can afford it might visit Internet cafés. Home Internet use is not common because it is more costly and unreliable.

Sports

Football is the most popular sport in Iraq and the Iraqi national team has been nicknamed 'Osood Al Rafidayn', which means 'lions of the two rivers'. In 2007, the team defeated

FAMOUS IRAQI

Kadim Al Sahir (b. 1961)

Some people call Kadim Al Sahir the 'Robbie Williams of the Middle East'. This Iraqi pop star is known for his poetic lyrics. He was trained at Baghdad's Music Academy, and has sold more than 30 million albums all over the world. In a BBC Radio 3 poll of the world's top songs, a song by Al Sahir was voted number six.

Saudi Arabia to win the Asian Cup for the first time. A total of 24 teams tried to qualify for the tournament, and like the UEFA Champions League, 16 teams eventually competed. The Asian Cup is held every four years, and Saudi Arabia, Iran and Japan have each won the cup three times.

Economy and trade

Each year, Iraq sells about US$42 billion worth of products to the rest of the world. Oil makes up the largest proportion of this, and accounts for about 84 per cent of Iraq's income. Iraq only uses about 15 per cent of the oil it produces – it exports the rest.

PLACE IN THE WORLD

Value of economy: **US$60.12 billion**

Percentage of world total: **0.14%**

World ranking: **63rd**

Income and spending

Iraq spends roughly US$48 billion each year, which is about US$6 billion more than it earns. The country has to spend this money to buy goods for its people, which must be imported from other countries. Iraq's main imports include food, medicine and manufactured goods. Roughly 30 per cent of Iraq's imports come from Syria. In addition, 20 per cent of imports come from Turkey, 10.8 per cent from the USA, and about five per cent each from Jordan and China.

▶ *These farmers are gathering hay in northern Iraq. About five per cent of Iraq's economy is made up of farming.*

▲ *Iraqi workers lay down the last row of bricks on a wall at the Central Euphrates Farmers Market in Haswah.*

Trade with other countries

Iraqi-made products such as chemicals, cloth and leather account for about eight per cent of its exports. Most other Iraqi exports are agricultural products, such as wheat, barley, rice, vegetables and dates. Iraqi farmers also grow cotton and raise cattle, sheep and poultry. Iraq's main import partners include other countries in the Middle East such as Iran, Syria, Turkey and Jordan. Because these countries are nearby, it is easier for them to transport goods into Iraq. Major oil-consuming countries such as the USA, Canada and Spain are key export partners. Around 40 per cent of Iraq's exports go to the USA; another 13.7 per cent go to Italy, and about five per cent each go to Spain, Canada, France and the Netherlands.

Rebuilding

Despite continuing violence, Iraq is making progress in rebuilding the country, especially in the safest areas. It has airports, roads and transport systems to help move goods in and out. It is also working with other countries to reduce the money it owes them.

IT'S A FACT!

More than US$100 billion of foreign aid is helping rebuild Iraq after many years of war. This is more than in any other country in the world. The money is used for reconstructing damaged buildings, as well as education and healthcare.

The Central Bank

Iraq's Central Bank is the key to its future economy. The Central Bank is like the Federal Reserve in the USA or the Bank of England in the UK – these banks work closely with the government to keep prices from rising, so people can afford to buy food and energy such as electricity. They root out bad practices and cheating in order to keep their country's economy moving. They also help to build other banks and try to find money to lend to people who want to start a new business. A strong economy with banks and businesses is important if Iraq is to become a more powerful country.

Working together

In May 2007, the Iraqi government created a document that outlines its aims for the country's future. Iraqis hope that by creating partnerships with other countries, Iraq will become a bigger part of regional and global economies. The Iraqi government is now passing laws to make the economy stronger.

One law is a revenue-sharing law, which will allow income from oil to be equally distributed between all regions of Iraq. Another is a hydrocarbon law, which will help Iraq find new ways of developing its resources beyond oil, to greener forms of energy.

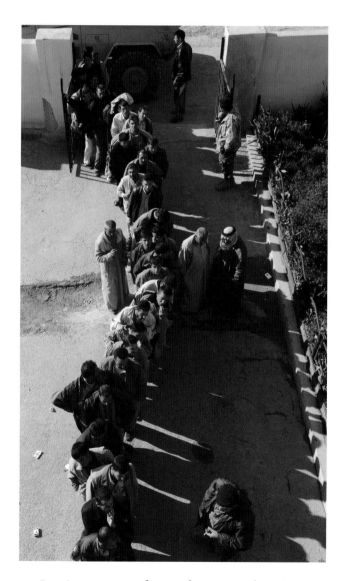

▲ *Iraqi men queue for work on a road repair project in Nimrud, in December 2008. Hundreds of men applied, but only 192 could be employed.*

IT'S A FACT!

The unemployment rate in Iraq fluctuates between 18 per cent and 30 per cent, while Iraq's neighbour Kuwait has one of the lowest unemployment rates in the world – just 2.2 per cent.

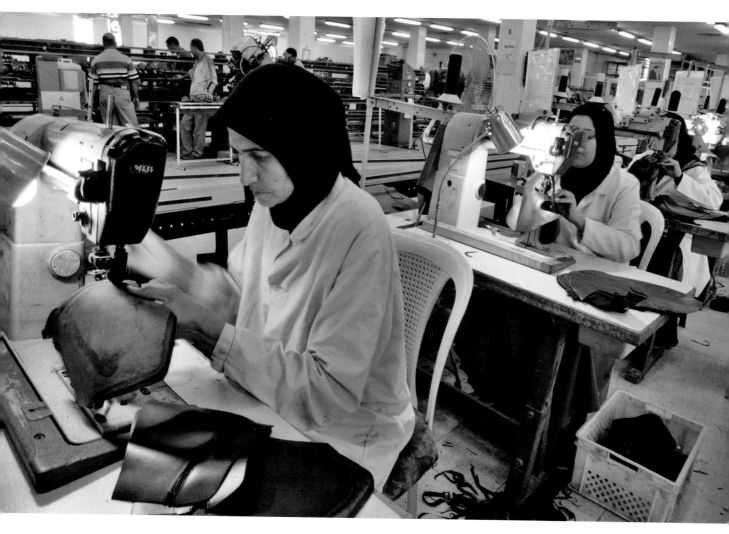

▲ *These Iraqi women work in a large sewing factory in Baghdad.*
Women are being trained to work in all kinds of jobs in Iraq.

Services and manufacturing

Services, such as banking and government, account for nearly half of Iraq's economy and employ almost half its workforce. Manufacturing mostly revolves around the oil industry. However, Iraq also has important chemical, textile, construction and processed-food industries that all benefit its economy.

The role of women

In the past, Iraqi women were less likely to be employed than men, but today as many as 1.5 million Iraqi women are undergoing training to gain new employment. They study at 17 vocational technical training centres and 28 employment services centres throughout Iraq. The women are being trained in jobs such as teaching, nursing and manufacturing.

Iraq's government is one of the youngest in the world. In the years since the fall of Saddam Hussein, Iraq has formed a whole new system of government. Based in Baghdad, it includes a prime minister – who is the head of government – and two deputy prime ministers. Iraq also has a president and two vice presidents. The rest of the government is made up of representatives from a number of different political parties.

IT'S A FACT!

In the current administration in Iraq, there are four women cabinet members, including the minister of state for women's affairs, the minister for human rights and the minister for environment.

Voting

Iraq's first democratic election in more than 50 years took place in 2005. All Iraqi citizens over the age of 18 were allowed to vote. In Iraq, there were terrorist threats during the election. Some people feared there would be widespread violence, but even though there were some attacks, most Iraqi voters safely went to the polls to choose their leaders.

◀ *This Iraqi hospital worker proudly raises her ink-stained finger. The fingers of Iraqi people were marked with ink to show that they had cast their vote.*

A new government

Iraqis voted for 275 members of a National Assembly. The National Assembly then drafted a constitution and selected the country's leaders. At least one-quarter, or a minimum of 69 members, of Iraq's Council of Representatives must be female. In the elections of 2005, 85 women were elected. In comparison, only 18 per cent of members of parliament in the UK are women.

▼ *Iraqi officials celebrate the new constitution, a first step towards a new Iraqi government.*

GOING GLOBAL

People aged 18 and over who were born in other countries to Iraqi citizens were allowed to vote. Some of them had never even been to Iraq. Voting in the 2005 election took place in 14 countries besides Iraq – Iran, Jordan, Turkey, the United Arab Emirates, Syria, the UK, Sweden, Germany, the Netherlands, Canada, France, Denmark, Australia and the USA.

Iraq's constitution

Later in 2005, Iraqis voted again – this time on a constitution, or set of rules for the country. Most countries have a constitution that lays out the basic rights of the people. No laws can be passed that go against a constitution. For example, although Islam is the national religion of Iraq, other religions can also be practised and no law is allowed that stops people from practising a religion. The constitution promises that Iraq will look after its people, it seeks to keep Iraq safe, and it states that it rejects violence and wants to stop terrorism.

IT'S A FACT!

More than 25 countries in Asia and Africa recognize Islam as their official religion, including Iraq's neighbours Iran, Jordan, and Kuwait.

The Arab League

A regional organization of Arab states was started in 1945. Since then it has included Egypt, Iraq, Jordon, Lebanon, Saudi Arabia and Syria. Today, the Arab League has 22 member states and it represents 314 million people. Like the European Union, it aims to create closer trade relations among its members. It is also a political organization that works to settle disputes among its members. For example, in August 1990, 12 of the 20 voting Arab states disapproved of the Iraqi invasion of Kuwait.

Foreign relations

Iraq is working hard to re-establish its relationship with other countries. It has representatives in 54 countries around the world, including a representative to the United Nations in New York. A total of 43 countries have their own representatives in Iraq.

◀ *The new Iraqi constitution promises to protect its people, and Iraqi troops work with other peacekeeping troops to keep the streets safe.*

▲ *Although relations with the USA are improving, there is still tension in Iraq. These Iraqis are holding a peaceful demonstration against the US presence there.*

Iraq and the USA

Despite the US invasion of Iraq in 2003, the new Iraqi leaders and the USA are now working together to promote peace in the future. In 2007, they signed a Declaration of Principles, which set out the terms for a future relationship between the two countries. The US has agreed to have a long-term relationship with Iraq. It has committed to helping the country form and strengthen its political and economic systems, and it has also agreed to help train and arm Iraqi security forces to help keep the country safe. It is hoped that good relations with the USA and other nations will secure peace for Iraq.

Iraq is a country with an ancient history and a troubled past. Its people have faced decades of cruel leadership and wars, families have been forced apart and many homes have been destroyed. Ancient landscapes and holy sites have been permanently scarred.

What does the future hold?

No one knows or can predict what Iraq will be like in 2020. The country may have a promising future, face even more troubles or remain much the same. But no matter what happens, there is no disputing that Iraq and its people have suffered great damage. It will take a long time to rebuild the country. Steps are being taken to improve Iraq, however. For example, the marshlands are being restored, and the Marsh Arab people are moving back. Kurdistan is gaining recognition and may become an independent country.

▼ *These Iraqis are begging for food in 2006. Since then, the quality of life for people in Iraq has improved, and it should continue to do so.*

A changing world

As Iraq changes, so too does the rest of the world. Countries such as the USA are hoping to become less reliant on oil from other countries, including Iraq. This could greatly impact Iraq's future because most of its exports are oil-related, and its biggest customer is the USA. Oil is also a non-renewable resource, and it will eventually run out, so Iraq must find other ways of improving its economy.

The people of Iraq

Most people living in Iraq today believe the country is heading in the right direction and feel positive about the future of this young country with an ancient history. Iraqis carry many challenges in making their country strong again. Many simply want to live in peace, enjoy time with their family, and see their country grow and progress in a positive way. That is exactly where much of the world hopes Iraq's future lies too.

▲ *Iraqi children smile through a hole in a war-damaged building.*
As reconstruction projects get underway, schools will reopen and children
may be able to play freely in the streets again.

Glossary

civilization a developed society that has political and social groups as well as arts and sciences.

confined to be kept inside a certain place.

constitution a document that lays out the main laws of a nation. Laws are not allowed to be passed that contradict a country's constitution.

continents the Earth's seven great land masses – Africa, Antarctica, Asia, Australia, Europe, North America and South America.

descendants people born from relatives who lived before them.

economy the financial system of a country or region, including how much money is made from the production and sale of goods and services.

ethnic relating to a specific group of people with the same background.

export to transport products or materials abroad for sale or trade.

immigrants people who leave their own country and come to live in a new country.

import to bring in goods or materials from a foreign country for sale.

Islam a religion with belief in one god (Allah) and his last prophet, Muhammad.

Islamic Empire a series of empires that were based on the religion of Islam and ruled over much of Asia, Africa and Europe from around CE 700 until 1918.

landlocked surrounded by land – with no borders on seas or oceans.

migrating moving from one place to another.

nomadic a lifestyle that involves moving from one place to another instead of settling in one place.

pilgrimage a journey to a holy place.

political parties groups of like-minded people who seek power or representation within a government.

prophet a person who is revered as being a direct representative of God.

republic a political system whose head of state is not a king or queen, but a president who has been elected by the people.

reservoirs human-made or natural lakes used for storing water.

resources things that are available to use, often to help develop a country's industry and economy. Resources could be minerals, workers (labour) or water.

textiles cloth or fabric, usually made from weaving or knitting.

Further information

Books

Ancient Iraq (Eyewitness)
by Philip Steele
(Dorling Kindersley, 2007)

Iraq (Countries in the News)
by Simon Ponsford
(Franklin Watts, 2006)

Iraq Then and Now (Middle East)
by John King
(Raintree, 2006)

Saddam Hussein and Iraq
by David Downing
(Heinemann, 2004)

Websites

**http://news.bbc.co.uk/cbbcnews/hi/specials/iraq/
default.stm**
Children's BBC Newsround Iraq page.

**http://www.cyberschoolbus.un.org/infonation/
index.asp**
United Nations website information about all countries
for children.

**http://teacher.scholastic.com/scholasticnews/
indepth/war-iraq**
Scholastic News page all about rebuilding Iraq.

**www.timeforkids.com/TFK/specials/iraq/
0,8805,424876,00.html**
Time for Kids: America at War, with information about
the US presence in Iraq and what the future holds.

*Every effort has been made by the publisher to ensure
that these websites contain no inappropriate or offensive
material. However, because of the nature of the Internet,
it is impossible to guarantee that the content of these sites
will not be altered. We strongly advise that Internet access
is supervised by a responsible adult.*

Index

Numbers in **bold** indicate pictures